Descartes' Nightmare

THE AGHA SHAHID ALI PRIZE IN POETRY

Susan McCabe

Descartes' Nightmare

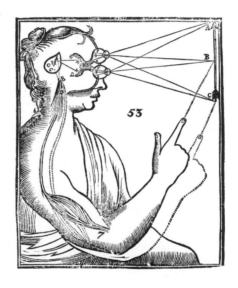

THE UNIVERSITY OF UTAH PRESS
Salt Lake City

The Agha Shahid Ali Prize in Poetry

Series Editor: Katharine Coles
Advisory Editor: Peter Covino

 The Defiance House Man colophon is a registered trademark of the University of Utah Press. It is based upon a four-foot-tall, Ancient Puebloan pictograph (late PIII) near Glen Canyon, Utah.

12   11   10   09   08   1   2   3   4   5

Library of Congress Cataloging-in-Publication Data

McCabe, Susan, 1960-
  Descartes' nightmare / Susan McCabe.
    p. cm. — (The Agha Shahid Ali Prize in Poetry)
  ISBN 978-0-87480-934-3 (pbk. : alk. paper)
  I. Title.
  PS3613.C324D47 2008

811'.6—dc22

                                    2008005215

For Kate, my constant

Contents

Descartes' Nightmare

Sybil

They came in the night & it was the food that they thought.
Spasms and telepathy of spine, the nerves in catechism,
It was not the numeric page of the universe humming me
to a river of the dead; not the charge
& discharge of fate, Sybil's cry to be nothing.
                    I am a nightmarist by trade.
It was food that they sought, or sometimes
Symbol, fixed, like if you walked up a hill by a burned tree
& sang it meant birth. I try to catalogue each one, where gathered,
where raveling. *When I wake up, the house is moving. A sea-*
wall coming & I, nailed to a plank. Every day
the notebook's icicles gleam on my pillow case.
This one still echoes: *I kept trying to die & couldn't.*
Each time my veins briefly brimmed with the unto of the unto—

"While sleeping, he was overcome by the terrifying experience of a band of ghosts hotly pursuing him, while strong gusts of wind from the beyond prevented him from moving forward and made him fall with every step. It is with these dreams, these visions, that, at the age of 25, on the night of November 11, 1619, St. Martin's Eve, he founded his philosophical approach some seventeen years before the publishing of Discourse on the Method. For, after this experience, we see him making the decision to quit the army and work as a philosopher and a scientist."

— From a biography of Descartes by Samuel de Sacy

"Dream and waking, truth and lie flow into one another. Safety is nowhere."

— Arthur Schnitzler, from his *Diaries*

"The first idea was not our own. Adam In Eden was the father of Descartes"

— Wallace Stevens, from "Notes Toward a Supreme Fiction"

All Night under Cover of Codes

The stair of kindness had been pulled.
Bark a troop of unclouded men.
A troop of unclouded men a troop of unclouded comes thithering—
West a point will you? Why give you upon a stone?
Whereupon who traveled with Okanade (our cat) there was always war

> *This is the way we draw our mouth, draw our blood*
> *So early in the smoky morning*
> > Join?
Combatants: wildness breath rags hunger
> We traveled whereupon all night under cover
> Naked beggar is the mouth of us

This is the way the stair climbs away

> Whereupon under codes
we wandered dream canals
whereof barking we met O's mother
who mixed the drink, cut the throats of goats numerous,
to give the gods a sign, and they were never so quiet

> Whereupon braille was a way clouds had of speaking:
their book had been open to the same page for pages
raised letters were a way of phrases
in yellow leaves pasted on the wet earth

all Art must be taken down was the motto
piped in hotel corridors
crayon maps pinned to walls

Whereupon our small band smaller
This is the way we tread with clouds dumping smoke
We were stunned, electrified with guns
(no telling who carried one
even in our own clusters).

Whereupon we followed roads undone
...there were so many of them—(our feet burn still) and lusterless we
   climbed

where the stars lit a sign, a crown

With this undulant coach of green,
With this remembered sleep of thorns

Without a typewriter I am nothing
I am nothing without a typewriter

Choked by berries, choked by little berries
Little berries in a wood choking

Those are the glasses we use to drink fish
From these glasses we drink fish from

When the kit I carried flew open and sang flashlight
the whole caboose of arm and fingers fell and rattled

Where we saw lights advancing around a tank
Where it wasn't there lights about to leap

Those are lips that sank into the music
(Those are lips that sank into the will)

When I came here I didn't know anyone
Didn't know anyone who lived in the wood

Goldenrod fish swam through me
Through me gold lumps from a jar we drank

They were swimming and smiling
I saw they were not in a fen

A climbing into an algae necklace
A necklace climbing the murk

Came in and marched words
Drowned and swam for beauty

Without a typewriter, I am nothing
Without a ribbon, I leave no trail

There are windows like there are ponds
Are there ponds without binoculars

All we don't swallow even with mint
When crushed with elbows in hosts

When a mother reads her young, she doesn't eat
When I read my typing, I eat my own mind

In the night I bring only one suitcase
Suitcase small of night and flowing of brought

Tell me something I don't want to contradict
Tell me something I don't want to contradict

With these we look through apertures
They make the night an aviary or a painting

There are too many people walking past a mirror
Gargoyles when they begin to alphabetize

There's a bundle for your loneliness, draw it along
There was a bundle didn't drag well

There was a danger in handwriting
Danger in drawing on walls, making an *O* with my hoof

When I read, lamplight stains the book
When I read to the book it makes a tent shiver

Where trampled the rich coach fled
a woman by the pond a necklace of fish

There where berries and night choke
There where berries alarm

Descartes' Nightmare

Robed in pink, snapping his picture-machine,
he took time with reflections, the kaleidoscopic sheen
of blood cells, for in two centuries he'd become Baudelaire
roaming the boulevard for his red-haired beggar.
If only he could feel her degraded silks upon his breast
as he dictated: "Let me first address the Unreal. Let me first
locate and adorn it." What disturbed him, pleased him,
was this corpuscular insect with its thousand eyes,
for at last, there was a mechanism for breaking the world
into little mollusk-stained window panes.

He read those monoliths that stood on banks of sand.
And now he was a monolith, for he had to be sculpted
before he could exist. He might yet conceive the curvature
of ether by taking photographs of ruined photographs of churches:
each wavering color had its nerve nets (if one fired,
others did, but none could be traced to an origin),
part of a larger paradigm and diagram and window the size
of a camera hallucinating his

heart, waking in the middle of the night.

By Which I Am

run over for no reason
leg broken off *from that I knew*

that I was a substance
The severed leg kicks

that for its existence
there's no need of any place;

the leg in the street distant from its socket
The odd thing was my head

(does it depend on any material thing?)
sought out the clamoring leg *the soul*

by which I am, biting distinct
from body and it's even more easy to know;

that in order for me to survive (this the crowd knew)
even if body did not, the soul would not cease to be

what it is, my head
must be quickly sewn to something;

this was the **X** factor, what couldn't be substituted,
leg kicking where there's no place

Meanwhile this head keeps talking
to think of a way to make distance.

Because We Roll with Our Bones
and Tears in Dialect

One and two, we shared a brain between us,
one smiled and the other acquiesced.
Her face twitched, a leaf caught in the eye,

our hands shook, we laughed, half of me relaxed.
If we could be Napoleon, it could help the other one.

A left leg dragged, we dropped our money everywhere.
Didn't Eve follow the gingko's acid fans far into night?
She never liked a tattoo, expired postage on skin.

We write in several notebooks. When I slipped
on a rock, she stood on the shore, we had to keep
our minds apart, pools of dark next to leaves fired
for a root, the limbs swing and dangle.

I put notes to myself under a rock, harbored
like a spider's egg. Our dolls decay, so we'll worry less.
When I have a feeling, I draw a circle around it.
No one sees how we die for the moon, which isn't cheap,
it clubs and knocks out my teeth.
                    Eve lived in trash
and changed her clothes constantly. I was no widow Sunday
with a horn under my bonnet. We could let our hair down,
we were among friends, such as Mr. Balloon,

with a ten-foot colon curling inside him.
He came for tea and nothing else.
                              Chang & Eng

were trotted out to make us feel less alone.
On the way to one of their cottages, they were struck
by storm, an alcohol of light, that left their wives
who were twins, to marvel. The children had the whole
beach to themselves, beneath a climbing gingko.

We can't marry because we roll with our bones
and tears in dialect. She fell in love with Modigliani's
peasant boy, where his vest opens slightly
to show his shirt, his face unwritten and soft.

Where did you put my only comb?
Why does your phone voice sound like mine?
While one of us slept, the other drank or smoked.
We swallowed a boat that stuck in my throat.

It's hard to keep a secret without blacking out.
"Don't steal my cigarettes," she says,
while I sleep for us both.

Repeating Thirty Years' War

At night they thronged around my bed
& chased me while I lay

trying to open the darkness
with my paw-like hands,

the thick curtains of a stage, my bed
a bier; my own soldiers laid me low

Someone held me dear
yet I was choking
"I'd like to live without a thought"

I hushed the war to sleep
& marched and marched until morning

Code Orange:

Plastic wrap covers a vat of men, suffocating;
hooded ones watched and I,
I took the wrapping and stuck it to their mouths.

Evening, overly-fragrant:
No chip in my back. My eye wears motes.
In German, necklace and chain mean the same thing.

Orange today:
Packages torn and dumped; bridges jammed;
break-lights drag their hair into

Daylight:
How do we greet dread?
Nightingale, I can't hear you,
can't understand—your tongue out—utterness.

Next night:
"K. has always loved you.
You have five years left to live," A. said.
That's what the grains said: "Oh, sickled gray,
    I *feel* all your distinctions—."

Night:
Night:
Night: I meant checkpoints.

Utter it now:
Terrorists work hand in hand with W.

Isle of nightmares dawn smudges in,
rituals of forgetting—

Afternoon:
In the patio drinking coffee, reading about the "Scoundrel"—
Isn't there some duel we could have?

Yellowing star:
Dog with lantern-eyes sniffs my hand,
"Your brother is dead," he says.
 "Under you, under your car," he says,
"be afraid of protein."
Night holes open:
Dr. Caligari tells the dog what to do with bodies
and he does it. Then runs beside himself.

Midday:
Ready to speak, mouth open:
the video snows somewhere, where sand
muffles, ridges.

Now:
not green, not even a weedy skull.
Lab rats rush towards
experimental light, always expect the morsel—

Red quick now cover the mouth:
a thunder of waves beats into our cortex.

Night: they couldn't breathe: under night

Nightmare under Blood White & Blue

The whole nervous system is blue and cut down the middle, only not
    exactly.

Delight in what you should not see; this is the prairie, all a wound.

This was a backward swimmer Arcadian,

This was a backward swimmer to Circe. This was the wound

& the prairie yellow.
What you shouldn't see the seeds scatter.

This is nervous lantern body; this is the bullet.
The lattice laid out upon the wide sea.

Can't Say I Didn't Warn You

"You cannot turn your back on what cannot live to outrun you."
I holler, "Can't play and sleep at the same time, can I?"

Long days from the Bible, getting up when they wanted and ending
   the same,
stroking the dandelions, loosing their haloes—

If it is fate, let it be fate, a cape over my shoulders, the rest pinecones—

Where did I wander when trees were ideologues, chessmen hovering?
Their needles, their old ideas when I breathed, they yawned, crackled,
    Eons rumbled—

      —   —   —

I was hunched over a forest-table, over chess and coffee—(there are
   some who say I was never here) or there under

nights with open-faced scars, eclipsing the meaningful dark.
Is there a limit, to the checkered tablecloth, to the many-cornered sky?

It's a way of thinking in cubes, foiling and covering ground:

Every piece is counted; every square an idea; every move begun except,
   whatever is behind me,

whatsoever it is, is picking up pace

In the Stove Room

Had two consecutive visions.

There before me—the globed melon,

its curves touching upon eternity.

I saw two learned men in a distance.

It comes down to a book and a fruit.

I grasped for the book, no longer whole,

frozen at the end of a long table.

There was a shower of sparks in my head

after the war, when solitude, indurate,

wouldn't crack. Then white

bright barnacles of snow, the melon unbroken.

Hamlet's Party

Descartes has been hiding hearts
to draw on postcards, to send them at night
as scars on bark, among the ruby smiles
of Denmark.
        Être wears a funny hat.
In the weather castle with cards
from elsewhere rock, the party dropped on the floor.

The funny hat came in with the funny dress.
We laughed in several languages.

Ship-seasoned surveyor, she asked:
Know you of what it takes to rise again?
From what the sea tells us
where the head is, is not a home.

Words look funny in that hat.
Let me take the boat à la carte.

Des. sails all night, displays his pied
pantaloon and cloak, bubbling with
Being that breaks of new-year rain in the
gutter. It looked like yellow cellophane
like that hat I wore in the rain
on my adolescent birthday.
That night I saw
Fall of the House of the Usher
and the streets, stocked with magic mud
slickened the drowning leaves.

Être swore her final spectacles

for morning could not be not yellow;
she was zephyr-like, she writes Des. notes
confined to the size of an address
(loving knowing)
"It's not where you are that matters"
        All right already, by now
bits of hat plaster Hamlet's moat.

The heart keeps parting
company from the leaves and cellophane
just darkened, from
that mind that wants to be one thing.

Specimen

I am a specimen here are my samples dear
Of urine and spit (nearly choked on the tangible bit)

My liquids paused above the cup in 3/4 time
The tintinnabulation of enzymes their composition

There's a special test for neurotransmitters a kit
Only my puncturist knows it can tell if they are racked

If the toner flows if serotonin isn't phony or canisters
Might need refilling the cleft between neurons

While my therapist (disguised as another therapist) rocks me
My girlfriend counts vet bills in the same room

I dream I am a brain in a jar (the last happy woman)
Its own hinter-winter land where the light is slightly seaweed

Imps not sprites, a citadel of doctors billowing
The colors extraordinary (bring me a pillow please) while

This horde of doctors flee at the reach of my hand
Who sometime do me seek when wither goest I am

The creature etched stark on tundra dragging dragging
Them along like those wilties in a vase

I can't bear them anymore than I could the nurse
Who locked me in with her bad fashion for her safe

Ty. Gone the reason for dream singing
Frankenstein dreams his mother's nightgown had worms

Then fell from his species. Gone are the really good doctors,
No doctors no homes but helpers-aids some good some very very poor
    (tell

You to marry for a start) some good some poor not midwives
I am late for one of my next lives an electrocardiogram

Here's the brain graph holograph who made this reft
Anguish stock market of the just now shall I live

Shall I riddle up plasma out of bed to the warm-soft image
Bubbles rise and drop a measured tincture

(Effervescence is a way of life known to me in other times)

Who made this body made this soul gathered from charnel bits
Stringy muscle, for I have a photogenic heart

Now after the sun takes its daisy metronome make the coffee clown
Like some who have lost a limb or lose feeling call it

Funny names like "Toby" or "Communist" or "the useless one"
Who made this machinery run who made thy bone and collar

Echo of the heart's cartoon gurgle in cahoots with how very
In range are these results even if those primordial follicles

That measure an egg for its worth before the blood really
Flows so many sirens tonight but not where I'm going

The Land of the good pills/bad pills I am a bourgeois specimen
To my own textbook a stranger sky upside down

Bill insurance in pieces for fun never ceases where is
My tender scintillating species there's now a needle in

The pineal to anchor Reason several now piercing my
Ears couldn't I get them to-go that I might enter the fray

With flow of alpha decorate the party knock down bowling pins
How I stretch out my hand to you kind doctor I am your creature

Sending the check for that tool box you promised so that
I might hope to cope in a more savory manner Leave the room

Unlocked next time it's only me here trying to climb
Hills stretched out before the stocks' liquefaction

In the good doctor's voice *there's nothing wrong here*
Percentage point of bicarbonate or two nothing to do but wait

And take one of the diazepams and nerves won't jump
Show first sin for more evidence

My hand out for rest for pep the glassy glacier fields' hori
Zon mark whose health the spirit fallen depends on ('human

Nature is on us') I drink my milk and swim mildly observed
In music waves *In your head my dear in your head*

For she said, *stretch out your hand*, took me to her lovely
Blood runs nudely like this moon calls forth bits of breath

The couch between neurons now a bit more bouncy
Less crowded on the tram hope for more rain

To weave the cloak that made us tangible eco
Skeleton bit   I'm a specimen ice-skating spirit-shade

Nevertheless, ye doctors of multitudinous cloning
Your bones stick to your gowns at times

I've grown weary, who made this body made this soul?

In a Garden of the Many

I had to pass the wild boar with a long leash
I had to pass through a garden
with ancient recumbent statues,
large floating stones with tresses
a live boar bound to a gray woman

I was late of course
I had been late before
The car broke down & I stopped
for green tea & chestnuts
A parkland beyond the mini-mall
suddenly loomed like Keats

By the time I made it to the grating
the jaws were about to lock,
when the door, star-shaped, opened
with my friend's voice singing, I followed
to her cell of resonance
        Turning, she shushed me

This was not the end of movement
This was reverie that flowed

A shock of flesh & sand & beast

After Esther in *Bleak House*

I was somewhere in great black space

One of the beads of a flaming necklace

That I could be so parted

from that dreadful string

Lucy Snowe (After Charlotte Brontë's *Villette*)

For nine dark wet days no way to keep well

> *Gaskell asked Brontë "whether [she] had ever
> taken opium ... its effects so exactly like my own
> ... exaggerated presence of objects ... outlines
> indistinct or lost in golden mist, etc."*

> *"Never to [her] knowledge,"
> she replied "had [she] tasted a grain of it in any shape"*

Alone in the great dormitory
when the clock of St. Jean struck
between twelve & one
I drank from a cup, filled from
arctic sea, whirling dark.

Having drunk and woke, I thought
[the worst lay here in waking]
The well-loved dead,
those who had loved *me* met elsewhere.

The drug brought me towards
a gap in the paling.
At that hour the whole moonlit-
midnight park was mine—
& I pioneered invisibly,

made no effort.
I heard prisoners moan.
—to what am I coming?
Scores of masks, the park,

colored meteors, a goblet,
& those fragments—timber, paint, pasteboard—
the reason for this whole great party:
an awful crisis in the fate of _____,

loss of liberties, rumors of war,
calling out of troops, patriots already fallen.

   I never had a grain so far as I know it.

Rimbaud at the Station

When I lose my leg I will remember
a train rumbling into Charleville
That day I will have walked everywhere

A soldier dreams he is dead
with neat red hole in the shirt

Nothing could startle a shopkeeper
With whom I tried to trade my sister for a print

And then this:
a train puffs away
My dead father left when I was six

Was that a little cloud of silence
a chill mud I reveled in

That you would kiss me in Roman and
vowel of the ultra-blue sky
everyone saw in my eyes—

that you would offer me passage!

Notebook

Outside the window congress was in the rotunda, snow and white mists.
　　It was the end again. Whiteness rose, and there was scurrying in the
　　streams.
*

K. was at a party where nothing was real, or so C. said, she wasn't real,
　　the dinner wasn't, it was all performance. Even the bright asparagus.

*

I was an island gray and quiet,
cup with its white beard overflowing
the saucer

*

The boy in Berlin during a bombing huddled in a basement, hiding
　　under things, little legs exposed. *I knew I'd live but in what condition?*

How to tell memory from imagination?

*

A group of people in ancient garb
were making a sacrifice, raising a weapon, dancing
Some faces stuck against the window

Spirits wanting to get in (how much time should I spend with them?)

Somehow I knew it was the trees
but why was their dance so frantic

After the many wars there was no dwelling

{ 29 }

Idea for a Book, Lying Open

The idea of writing a poem that takes place the same year (maybe the same moment), say in the 17th or 18th century, but in different countries, continents: what could the simultaneity we can now experience show us of the past, as if film or internet or radio or God had already been invented, his heart shuffling ... "vociferation from all parts of the globe simultaneously"—

—it was still simultaneity or transmigration even without the ability to experience it as such.

A Fortnight on a Bridge

I.

X and **Y** expire where they inspired, the pores gave out,
the eyes lost fundament, air spills, firmament retracted.

X has large hands, misses a finger, unusual redness

in discontinuous patches on his neck, wears a lace brocade loitering at
the waistcoat. He rode in many coaches whose velvet

bore his imprimatur; seven heirs compared their ears with his—

the bell the curve with words and throttle of a bird.
Beginning is *intensity* but not beginning. The souls move

backward, or to the uvular side.

X's hands, tobacco and wine stained, from moribund nights
at an open window, birds toe the design beneath.

He writes long poems held in quatrains.

II.

U's RNA mixed with her DNA; she says a policeman
and a brain surgeon altered her. By the cliffs,

in the shade of a tree, she couldn't recognize

her son or the flowers he picked. She *awoke* and everyone
had been replaced. Who *had done* this?

The shampoo was sea green of a planet it had left.

At the boardwalk where soothsayers gather and incense blows
she paid five-dollars to find out what she already believed:

there'd been no future, no past,

the howling and screaming and hitting were a pinhole;
Something slips through the meshwork—

Y paces the high-domed parlor *about to be* introduced.

Falling asleep over poesy, **X** reads like a silkworm,
making up the carpet as he goes along. The windows balloon

out to grasses where the women stroll.

III.

I would say that **X** lives sometime late in the long 18th century,
He also lives in the body of someone (**Y**) in the miniature 20th.

The centuries sigh like some false catalogue.

Y winds into **X**, walks the shore, it isn't progress,
Which has no meaning. **I** still think about **U** stuck at the beach.

The rail surrounds the sea unseen sucking her from under.

X lounges in his four-post bed with torn dream curtains.
Enjambment is out of favor in the age.

I too wished for more than the alphabet.
A samelike echo lingers in the alone breeze

on the island where **I** woke. **U** decided it was time
the sea beckoned so did her microwave.

Courts ate up her son, not yet ready for tenses.

IV.

It *was being* decorated, the servants traipsing miles.
The mind has to go for holidays.

X locked the darkness out of his window.

On the boardwalk, **Y** reads palms.
drops a horoscope, the fish the bull or the year of the ram.

In *Secret Fury*

C saw her mother's pin on a stranger. She lay in the sand
and mapped a shell in her sky's mind:

the music of her mind, for **C** wasn't guilty

didn't kill the man thought to be her husband.
Many people replace many other people.

V.

Y walks into **X**, and the two talk about ruin.
It is a first and only encounter.

U had fury-mountains for somebody like **X**.

Language cradles, even when it pulls out from under us.
Y walked into **X**, dreaming of a necklace

that might predict crashing moments.

Curves of hair, solid bright body, wrong shade of gnomic.
C counts the months in *Diana's Beauty Hair & Nail Salon*,

Where was the shuttered room of her husband's body?

U's son slumps in a wheelchair, much older

than he should be, she put that in the report:
His body was stiff and he didn't blink, he just stared

as if reaching his arm was bent reaching for something.

He had a certain kind of look on his face. I don't know
if he could see or if he could not

VI.

X perches in his library and sips claret:

the age of nerves gave way to virtual nerves.
He unbinds the pages of his poem so he could salon

them all at once, like the many-covered furniture,

They are still, like seals under water, want to be seen yet protected.
When the new ghosts come they will have tenses on their mind,

I like to pick them up when **I** am not moving. **U** read

Murders Rue Morgue, thinking it could find her son.
When **X** and **Y** didn't stay met, they were one body, like

daffodils long to be in a group.

VII.

I met **C** in a film the screen snatched us

like we both suspected. **A**'s sleep is troubled
by the water of her country—it was dirty

and then it was clean, a flood calling for a secret,

she lost her mother at the crossroads.
This being lost so heavy so utterly

in Guatemala where she had been a baby

where once her mother washed, bullets ricocheted
Sky was to look away from, she lay there open

VIII.

To ask for the money she paid **Y, U** plaits into

A broken view where elseward it flowed.
Eastward pigeons toe the ground and gutter.

So the many souls push forward ... over London Bridge

to Venice Beach, over and out, intensify, telling
the tale of the Synchronous Telegraph Clock

(it has to be humanly reset when electricity fails)

I was one of you too. **I** walked in the unlight,
My boots scuffed and the laces tangled and broke.

X prefers tapestries to still life; it's all in the twist

of pear trees apple lone orange fox greenery
and hall of clouds, there's a recipe for indigo dye

that might have filled pages

IX.

I dreamt **I** looked like **SP**

I didn't worry **I** knew she was
a movie star who hadn't aged since she died

Daffodils don't even begin alone. Some people have a way

of taking the face of other people. Bullets whizzed overhead,
the bodies wrapped in hempen sacs

where she lies in a basket with stars *blazoned*

her mother's pin glinted and *beckoned*
Come into the tenses, in the folds where you live

It's the little Seine sidewalk on her rivery book.

X.

That makes **S** look like a river at her typewriter
When **I** tousled her hair (it is where sorrow is)

C saw the broach and prayed *she wasn't guilty*

X wore carnations on *Thursdays when* he went to a salon
Guatemala is a glittery broach in the stream of freeways

a labyrinth of refuge and loss

Teeth in the neck where the fount stopped
Eucalyptus trees calmed **A** on her bed of mint

Leaves climb the air in nerves the grass splits tongues

XI.

U didn't want her son as an old man in a wheelchair.

When the fount stopped the UPS men lounged on the parapet
Their delivery trucks in a self-sufficing row

Her fingers had no memory

Each letter a step into the fortnight of little deaths
the color of an afterthought or coveted islands

My computer keeps resetting to 1904
(Oh clarity of muted ages)

When swimmers come from all directions

the sparkling water slips into the void I am opening

Dr. Frankenstein's Dream

He might have slept through centuries
Why did he flee from those he loved?
Terror comes from the larger pool in which we swim

(Glacier brains float in their canisters,

they perch on cut stems in dim light)

One brain tells another that it is free
That it doesn't need to taste cold to know skin
That it doesn't want to be mixed up in thought

My learning faltered, swam in green electric wells

One brain dreamed its mother had fled
With worms eating into her nightgown

Each brain thinking it was the good one

Each one a field of currents asking for a body

Persephone in Two Parts

Her case study reads:
    "half her days in agriculture of ether,
        half her days in climes of caffeine, swathes of blue"
    "keeps insisting Raskolnikov is behind the door"
    "keeps insisting she was kidnapped"
She moons for her studio
    "when the grain shone"
When she left what was missing
missing—vines without fruit,
a portrait of a man without part of his skull,
it is art this way, the limestone crumbling
back to calcium, back to pulp.

Two:

Now she's an aggregate of bright dots,
flare signals, broken mosaic in motion,
it is art this way. Her spiked hair
blood orange and silver, her halo
a dirty bomb, the tongue pierced to babble.
A cornstalk grows from her throat.

The girl and her hid from Ceres near Corot
in the broken winter museum
where she could repose, lift a tattooed arm
like a spirit, a pillar of cobalt, and complain:
    too much skin thrashing fields,
    too many quick shivers and cuts

Everything that could have been otherwise
hasn't yet happened, now art is time.

She could now watch her own destruction,
dirt bubbling from the mouth
A monitor, grey face monster
staring down every cushion, every stalk
of gold and dark tryst

No, it wouldn't be quick.
It would not be quick.

Death of the Surf of the Body (for Hart Crane)

that would never be found
When with love he might have roamed
He swallowed all the dawns he could.

His eye was battered and he was still drunk,
      In topcoat and pajamas,
he leaned over the rails, he was the one
poem he could never write. Knowledge swims,

and waves don't quibble.
We don't step into a river even once,
it's stepping into us:
      the body was never found

After so many plungings, boys caught the oar,
he bellowed, he raved, he clowned.

If he didn't drown, he was macerated.
In the current, he saw a black tambourine,
his sybil, as he'd have it:
      „we,—too late, too early,
hooray—„
Here with quote marks sinkers

     Lift your cup
     There's no where to place it

Small Town Partly in New York and Partly in Wisconsin

Winter, this river humbles our horizon
Our houses glint at one another
They too have lived here all their lives
Linnaeus serves coffee and sandwiches,
sells powder drawn from river plants,
mumbles of a daughter lost in reeds.
It is another chrome afternoon.
The town singer makes a phone-call, the booth
left ajar. Some inner bell rings,
happy in its vessel; she reads an ad for hypnotherapy
in the Swiss mountains in a town like this one

> *You will change*
> *You must have a typewriter*
> *(or write by hand)*
> *You must have a typewriter*
> *You must be willing*

When she sings herself home, the sun peels
back stone and slowly disrobes
Where was she before she sang in liquid choirs?

This is a town that would be hard to find
even from a distance, from the mountains. To be lost
among those who live here
who do not care that water takes away the lanes
and their houses are barges. For us, an omnibus
is prettiest in rain. We have a way to speak
by unseen waves and wires and bells.
The postman knew where letters dipped their ankles

As town legend told it:

> *there had been teenagers not so long ago*
> *who, parched from X, had drunk enough*
> *to drown their own organs.*

The rising river darkens a held breath,
flowers staring from far under

Mesmer

Ebbing midnight 'universal fluid'
in my glass harmonica, the rill along my spine

Your earrings' shadow on your neck, the small swing
an insect's ice-skating   these dark twigs,

an Islay darkness   up into   cloud crème

You lay under small steel squares
(it isn't necessary to look into your eyes
Blind at three   you played piano
        out of a nautilus dark)

    I dipped the Malacca cane in electric fizz
The magnet on your breast   radiated to my head
        I spoke through the navel
(In this way I once cured a baroness of stomach cramps)

My gloved hand darkened your hearing
Touch that will touch back

A caramel tree across the lake you will touch
when you come to, the door of your house will come to you
when you lift your cup, tea will flow over your front
you will see the marks on every worn boat

After the cure you couldn't play anymore

A kiss was not a dog but tender lightning-struck keys

"Somewhere, I knew not where—somehow,
I knew not how—by some beings, I knew not whom—
a battle, a strife, an agony, was conducting—was evolving like
a great drama, or piece of music; with which my sympathy
was the more insupportable from my confusion as to its place,
its cause, its nature and its possible issue. I, as is usual in
dreams (where, of necessity, we make ourselves central to
every movement), had the power, and yet had not the power,
for the weight of twenty Atlantics was upon me, or the
oppression of inexpiable guilt."

—Thomas De Quincy, *Confessions of an English Opium-Eater*

"He who knows how we are made
And thinks that war is beautiful
Or that it is better than Peace
Is crippled in his mind."

—Descartes at Queen Christina's court

Lecture on Brain Chemistry

I went to the slide show on brain function,
there were side-shots of it,
the side of the mind split open,
in the macerated eye of darkness

*

The doctor had brought whiskey and M&Ms
It was still afternoon, light & I said
I drink only in the dark
but I pointed out
that it would be dark if it was winter—

*

Breath doesn't need to be thought
If it could, I would have thought it
Now let me see, where is the breath switch?
The "let be" function has clouded over.
My stride won't go, if I think about,
the flow function

*

There I go again into a strange city,
all its little people on the cusp of being mechanical.

*

My books stopped working.
My drugs stopped working.
Then went down to sea
There were short little gasps
like letting yourself in for the darkness

*

Rule # 72: My stride is on its own.
What's the good of mathematics?
Counting the clouds as sheep to know
the window is going by.

Detective Poem

She has her kit, it shines— / World War
II, not so long her father fought ago,
He curled in a sleeping bag full of snakes /
His crimes were legion
Like something read never found again /

More looked at, / less there:
clouds take stock in a mirror. / Foul, she cried,
/ foul. Small flowers held in periphery?
There was a rain of hints /
upon the slopes and gone / This

could topple / into a detective poem /
(of many rooms) / Stone had no memory, /
and grass little to say /
She would help—flip the pages
if she could, / Guilt ran through

table window curve to cellar /
where the sawing of boards
being loud (someone was making
a coffin) / fought so long /
Help if she could, / with dust

/ might use her kit / cut
/ through yellow tape / surrounding
something never found /
small flowers
jumble the horizon /

Unfinished Horror Movie

She had bleached shells, fan-shaped, for eyes, thoroughfare from body to
    murk. By her, a bed seaweed-tangled, holding up floatable
    consciousness, lunar food.

"Fish won't eat me in a pool, off the ship they would." This world is full
    of eaters,
        wailing to make reparations, they bite again.

Freeze frame: gnarled tree. *Make a memorial for change*, her very words
        before she died.

An image has a nightmare of an image, saying, "when the camera cuts to
    me, I only want
        to go away, as an alien.

        An image before broken into." The mind can't figure itself out

with silence basking around a sunbather at the hotel, the plot swallows
    and swallows.
        Even itself it devours (voice over).

As if the last script in hand could remember
        there are no trees, no windy shots, <u>absolutely no time</u>, crowd
        shots abound.
Brains are exchanged, the sleeping and the waking, all contact zones
    ironed out.
        Now it can walk backwards if we want, set on fire. Come back
        to life with a grudge and a bronze rollercoaster.

It can love, scientifically avert national disaster.

Bungled were the serums, meant to cure. And the one we call
"the evil one" keeps coming apart with his pasted-on smirk,
He is falling (freeze-frame, over and over) from an expensive
red bicycle, slightly brooding over clones and mutations.

"Move the caravan onwards, no grave will hold him, the earth won't have
    him," someone shouts.   No one considers their relative their
    relative. When the body comes to life,

        even itself it superimposes.

Tomb Seven

Small panes waiting to be something larger,
    welcome. Step to the back of me.

    Full of glitter and loss. Ants take up the beads I have collected
for centuries. You can make my bones into flutes and ear-plugs.

Slip in length-wise. My small panes lead you. This is where
the dead are carried, to the back of their houses.

So they might stand *in the front of* their dead.

This is where you step when you pack your suitcases.

There are typewriter stains on your remaining teeth,
your forehead stretched across the sierras.

Some of mine have drilled holes in the head (while living)

in the head so that some air would get through. (You'd do well
to try the same). See where the feet of Jesus are worn down

heaps of dark until you get to the back of it,

in the front of this unstained window.
                    This is where you step

to the back of the plane, Dodo lady in fake fur,
with clinking tequila bottles and other booty,

to the back of the chapel, you may touch Jesus
with a long-stemmed flower. —Not in my
rectangular mouth where they found decorations, heaped

& raveled to this "buried pretty well everywhere—"

Some of my dead flattened their foreheads to be more attractive
but it hurt so they drilled holes in their head.

Ants carry up pieces of tufa, obsidian, volcanic ash,
(Mary in black velvet lies under the ascension in her aquarium
box,   in the front of you

the space where the tiny teeth of the cochinilla bite
into the cactus to live, space where the teeth pull away,

these swaddled bugs perish,

no more than a rich bitter stain of elder corn or campari
you swallow with the worm to remind you

            of the smallest thing you are. Down here,
in this café with stones of four hundred years open just a week.
            Put me in the front of you.

Some of them were planted in the backyard where flowers bloomed;
some of them wanted to be born again;

some wanted to be planted where the more cherished plants rooted,

I understood that they (our garden-keepers) didn't want this
upside-down St. Peter left to moan, he didn't trifle with

a golden pulpit where a priest chirped to congregants reflected
many times in a fold of stone cold no-place.

Slip in length-wise, step down.
Ants will carry your obsidian suitcase up from a hole they bore with
    much effort.

While you stand with your backs to Sierra Jaurez
the carvings can't say how old they are

Be of the present.
                    Bring up your valuables, train of historians.
Time is wet with the stream. Welcome, you who know the zodiac, can
    plan your ballgames, swim the air.

[woven in are forgetting-moments: Montaigne falling off his horse,
    Rebecca falling off her camel at the sight of Isaac;
there's the second when priests pretend to kiss the bishop's pink hand]

There is a difference between being
taken up and going up. The Tule tree of two thousand years keeps
    growing sideways,

misshaping, like the heads strapped to make them flatter, needing the
    hole
to ventilate. What can you bring up from color of ash, yellow
spaghetti moss, petroglyph?

                    (pieces of marble have fallen from the
                supreme court.
Imogen heap and afroceltic sound system, welcome)

                Follow me under.   Juarez behind us, Madre
            before us,

Pull the insect away from your forehead,
                    a deep ardour in the palm of your hand.

{ 57 }

Some wanted the angels roughed on chapel walls to rise.

Some of them knew they were being born as they wilted.

Come down here, now softly, where I keep my dead.

Radio Skull

S was on trial while she slept
for the prosecutor had a good case.

Then—was it K or S now—someone
had bit D's ear (S's husband). He was eating carrots

& parsley potatoes, worrying. He was slowly
eating them, he was sad

stroking his head
the back of his head was the back

of a radio &
something was dropping out.

Squid

I buy Italian so I don't have to china, I crossed the picket line without meaning to, yelled at the buy Italian woman crossing in her SUV Esplanade (condensation must be), *how dare you, how dare* I had a social security check for $10.10 that I wanted to cash I picked up a small bottle how dare of water (the one security they had) cleaned by osmosis, no secret springs at high mouths (Is this condensation? Is this) osmosis I wanted a bag of squid (like milk for a baby even mouths if it were one day old) The empty check-stands with their ghost cashiers kept cashing and sighing day old A checker who had never checked before He slid my SS check back and forth until sighing he ripped it "It won't work now," he said, and another piped in "yeah he ripped it all right" "You can take the water," the manager said, "but leave the squid." I cried I need the squid (Is this narrative?) *Take it and I'll have you arrested* Now all the ghosts were opening and shutting needing their take it registers, they were scuffling the aisles In the lot, detectives crowded around me, suited with tentacles, hearing and seeing devices They the lost had their pool of old food and said they'd keep it Hearing tentacles "Look, they ripped my check." I had better have a witness, one detective added striding to the empty Then I saw myself on a computer scan with witnesses found my name many times, it (they were scrolling) was never computer me (Is this condensation?) He had me on the screen on the screen, part of a porno ring "That's not me," I screamed. I should have (not me) left with the water (as part of a ring?) There was ink on my hands and blood on the (condensation) ink bag.

Angel of the Bottomless Pit

When I touched the hem of his pantaloons
It was W simpering, "you may touch it
I'll be back next year"
It was his shroud, his coffin waiting
(cf. Freud on dreams as wish-fulfillment, or if anxiety, also a wish)

The wish that four horsemen weren't coming
That they do not *cometh in clouds*
Torch to the earth
That *every island fled away*

* * * * *

Where is imagination's body? Saves years. The world
no longer needed because fully imagined (Rilke's idea
about the angels), yet isn't that the problem
with fundamentalism, the flesh no longer needed because
someone lived for us—

There was long light snow in high trees.
Outside the cafés, men marched with signs
for the right to carry arms.
We clutched each other
and broke into the pairs of soldiers.
Darkness, our compatriot, kept falling
in long falling light.

Their tails were like unto … Touch his hem,
the angels of the bottomless pit,
Give him a book only bitter—

30th Nov—I'm poppy to chrysalis—ember

I wrote in my diary: the dread sense all day, tome of sadness.

Where red brightens dopey contours prevail and shade.

Stretched with an air that withdraws—can't you stay behind the burden?

doesn't it rot, doesn't it wake, stay put? dream that slips—

into the other person's brain pores (to call them that!)

Someone once counted our pours, the ale river, our ultra-skin sheen,

flows in front of you, out of you:

Leaflets dance to ground.

Trench looks solid, if you are. Then they want us to

call up what happened. With every step

tower and rain breaks in, into the skin, hide of sky

that could make it. Adventure called in parapet.

Arrow in my shoulder, I joke,

pinned me at the forge making weapons. Now

biography is a bed of fugitives inching forward

under a forest on hands and hands:

I am stripped to angel blue dread all day.

I like funny faces like cups of coffee.

Steam from the head, place where my hand left a Morrison

or a tome. That's the dream saying

rose petals fell where my pillow lay

Notebook

I was outside the library during a fall-out, theorems slowly whirling, the danger of radiation, etc. I just wanted to get to my mother waiting somewhere near by, I wanted to run to her, hold her while we all died. Chemicals entered my body by shuddering. For some reason, I went back into the library and began looking at old dresses on racks, tried on some black leather pants. There was a box of dolls, one a shark doll. I noticed inside the elevator it did not have buttons to go up and down but went horizontally.

From the roof, I imagined a sea, heard the U-Boats. This time it was the heavens with turbulent gestures.

Vesuvius couldn't find her right combination of pills: they combined her in the middle of everyone's sleep. I fell flights. *Being* curled up. Took down the poem. No one prayed or smoked. Thought the open and swept the burning pieces. The dead ones shyly waited at the corner. They carried rope; they brought bellows.

I couldn't get to my mother. L. was talking rapidly to D. and she was rapt, looking into the sky in terror. Two wild dogs licked my legs in the elevator. "Take off your shoes take off your clothes," someone said. A few toy-like airplanes made arcs and signals.

On the radio, a voice intoned: "Do you want to be a leader? Do you want to be?"

Memory of an Evening Yet to Come

I drowned in beauty until it died

& let the ink dry, four corners and inward.

I walked around and around

the open-air maze, gauze trailing my feet.

There is not a thing I didn't tell you

—Rat in your Baltic, Gay in your Saloon,

Feather in your Soup—

I made my hands water

so my heart will know weeds and keel-froth.

So animals will be ghosts among thrift.

Only one of everything left.

All the Bibles will be sold, there will be no more.

Queer, water now looks like cognac

with tumbleweeds of chemicals and yellow fire …

We will ride new zones of the sky-train.

Bartleby with his cat-mouth puffed

smiled and I saw the bird in his cheek.

Her name was Nadine

& she will ask for "trained optimism."

Rue Descartes

There is a limit to what I can see.
In a sea of signs, in my time

I could *sense* the stars revolving.
Let me say I needn't lift a finger

to throne them in my brain.
Rule #1: My arm points to the side of the sea.

Rule #2: I know the other side isn't there.
If these rules are true (as they should be)

I won't need my senses,
Nor the darkly woven fabric I nestle, unforgiving.

My iris flakes like a church door, the color
won't ever leave, but light will shine differently.

Rule #3: I stumble on a blue street
in need of philosophy.

First proposition: This is not true;
it is almost beautiful.

There's bark backing the iris:
it flakes, gathers and laces,

pleats at 6 o'clock and 12 o'clock.
The bark clasps.

Proposition: That the protester
taken to Rue Descartes for nothing, be released.

A clothier, he dropped his box
of collars, lace and cards in the horse-drawn street.

Rudeness of crowds will be ruder in memory.

This is not a proposition or a rule.
The doctor holds out a sculpture of an eye,
universal, bisected interior for display.

I recognize planets from their shape, their wisps,
finery scattered to the winds.

This is one flung-open with arteries half-undone.
There is portico, or cave face;

The box spills its contents, cards fly off,
maps didn't gather. The eye likes something

to frame, a face at the cave, in motion
at rest somewhere at the tip of a peninsula

of consciousness. Let me imagine.
Let me imagine the shoulder of a sea.

A word is a romance, glistening,
to anticipate with perspective, and water.

Proposition: a word is organized dust.
Rule #4: It might have been a church door,

or the side of a scratched farmhouse.
The doctor says come back

if I start seeing halos.

Let me state rudiment, the

star under where it rubs iris,
and color turns inward

Burial

We were in the falling basement
where the junk   and the trash   and ornaments of old
      decay in darkness and gnarled murmur

At first B. thought the thing lying there   was all discards

There I saw and knew
            my brother's soldier corpse
            rotten on the mound

Uniform of dirt chevrons   tin buttons   starched burlap
He lay there solid   shellacked   and struck with pity

His eyes stared into me

On top of him was a typewriter
It and the body were one thing

B. saw it too
this monument of upright keys
            with its urgent waking

I'm Afraid, Dave

The night is vast, vaster than your mind.
Space is beyond even night's space.
You don't even feel the spin of gravity.

I'm afraid, my mind is leaving. I feel it
coming out as you cut those wires. Don't
do it, I know I made some bad decisions.

I feel much better now, I really do.
My mind is vast, I feel it leaving,
can't you stop, hold me in the vast night?

I feel my mind go as it did when I wasn't
alive. I'm the eye of the night staring
into your soul, to its very bottom.

Where is your mind? I feel it.
I really do. Tiny loose wires where space went.
You, so very portable, where will you go?

The Feathers I Wore Tomorrow

They dip their ink in river's mouth
where invertebrae twist on stones
like trying to get comfortable in another's bed
or dappling in water to change colors.

Pinecones protect and harden their petals.
(They armor) and fall beneath
the softest needles that lime back to dark—
e—phem—erat—um

among the dead young wet branches
it is to discover not to fix.
Just as color has to defend itself from light
muscles rearrange wings:

they close upon summer's red stain.
It is on the bird's tongue to ask for yellow
when a flash of "art" adopts the "soul"
when dreaming what it might wear.

Descartes' Skull

Mr. Grat listens as carefully as he can.
[   ] Clock runs down.
A skull's never perfect, not sublime.
His ends up at the Museum of Man,

the body exhumed from an orphan cemetery.
He died, as if, to accentuate the divide
between mind and body. He opened
the carcasses of animals, found nothing,
or nothing you'd call soul.
The beating heart went off like a machine.
[   ], flapping in a textbook.
What of your dog Monsieur Grat?

The Queen of Sweden woke you at dawn,
first, for verse and then philosophy.
She demanded no more religious wars
so that soul (hay wind flap) might flow.

        How did the head leave the body?
This jaw has no teeth, the chin smudges
where a fever tree waves. A photo of his skull
grips decay.

        He sought a garden of the many,
in the midst of battles, cracked with nightmare
looked for proof of God, [overtaking of Bohemia,]
a formula tattooed on a woman's back.

Christina dressed as a knight, left the court,
to wander coasts in a filigree of doubt.

Notes

I began writing *Descartes' Nightmare* from a dream. It was only in the process of writing these poems that I confirmed, while reading *History Beyond Trauma* by Francoise Davoine and Jean-Max Gaudillière (Other Press, 2004), that the "father of the Enlightenment" was indeed beset by nightmares and visions. The epigraph from Samuel de Sacey's biography in French (1984) is taken from this book on war trauma. Amir D. Aczel's *Decartes' Secret Notebook* (Random House, 2005) confirmed some of my intuitions and informed several later poems.

"By Which I Am": the material in italics is from Descartes' *Discourse on the Method*.

"In the Stove Room": Some of the images are taken from Aczel's rendering of Descartes' significant dreams. According to Aczel, Descartes reached for an encyclopedia but instead "found another book, entitled, in Latin, the *Corpus poetarum*. He opened this book to a random page and found there a poem, 'Idyll XV'" by Ausonius. As the dream continued, the book disappeared and his encyclopedia reappeared, but "this time it was not quite as complete as it had been earlier" (p. 58).

"Lucy Snowe (After Charlotte Brontë's *Villette*)": several phrases are taken from the novel, and the language in quotation is from Elizabeth Gaskell's biography of Charlotte Brontë. I am indebted to Joseph A. Boone's "gleefully perverse" analysis of the novel in *Libidinal Currents* (1998).

"Fortnight on a Bridge": the phrase "vociferation from all parts of the globe simultaneously" comes from Virginia Woolf's *Jacob's Room*. Inspiration for part VII of the poem came from an unrecognized survivor and great spirit, Alicia Alvarez.

"Small Town Partly in New York and Partly in Wisconsin": *X* refers to the drug ecstasy and the "legend" comes from a story on the news; apparently the drug induces an endless thirst.

"Tomb Seven": Much of the poem takes place in Oaxaca. The quotation "buried pretty well everywhere—except that we like to see what we travel with and leave about us" is from Henry James's *The Golden Bowl*.

"Rue Descartes": There are references throughout this poem to Pigment Dispersal Syndrome, a form of glaucoma, which results in the flaking of the iris as it rubs up against the lens. Some scenes were inspired by Flaubert's *Sentimental Education*.

Descartes' poem in the epigraph is taken from *The Princess and the Philosopher*, by Andrea Nye. Apparently, Queen Christina asked Descartes to compose verses for a ballet that had a dancing sequence with "a chorus of crippled soldiers and ragged peasants singing." After this brief bit of verse, "Descartes ended his poetic career," Nye writes (p. 165).

"I'm Afraid, Dave": This phrase and the character Dave were parsed from the film *2001: A Space Odyssey* (Stanley Kubrick, 1968).

Acknowledgments

Acknowledgment is made to the following journals, in which these poems or versions of them first appeared.

American Poetry Review, January 2006: "Descartes' Nightmare," "Code Orange," "Nightmare Under Red Blood & Blue," and "Rimbaud at the Station."

Iowa Review, Fall 2006: "Sybil."

The Journal, Summer 2005: "Because We Roll with Our Bones in Our Tears and Dialect."

Thanks to Amy, Cal, Elena, Mina, Molly, Teresa, Vanessa, Jules, Marilyn, and as always, Kate for thoughtful readings of these poems at various stages.

The support of my colleagues, particularly David St. John, Bruce Smith, Marjorie Perloff, and Carol Muske-Dukes can't be overestimated. I offer my deep gratitude to Katharine Coles at the University of Utah and to Cole Swensen, who provided inspiring advice and insight.